BEING THE ANCHOR

*Tips on How to Be a Successful and Effective
Administrative Assistant*

Angelica D. Williams

Foreword By: Bishop B.L. Owens, Sr.

I would like to express my gratitude to the many people who encouraged me through this project; to all those who provided support, talked things over, read, offered reviews, listened to me discuss it and assisted in the editing, proofreading and design.

Thank you to my parents-- Bishop Robert and Elder Edna Williams: I realize that if it were not for you both I would not be where I am today.

To my children-- Adrianna, Makayla and Makenzie: Thank you for putting up with Mommy and the countless hours spent working. Just as I did not understand it at your age, I pray that one day you will understand exactly why I do what I do.

Briggette: You are the reason I am still in church today. Thank you for coming to pick me up on Sunday mornings. Thank you for encouraging me, praying with me and praying for me. Your many years of "Being the Anchor" have helped me in my journey. Thank you for being so transparent and open with me and thank you for assisting in the editing process.

To my pastors-- Rev. Dr. A.L. Owens and Bishop Brandon L. Owens, Sr.: Thank you for seeing in me what I could not see in myself.

Pastor Tawonna Kelly: You posted a comment on Facebook one day that pushed me to write. That comment was *"stop being so over dramatic and write that book"*. I never acknowledged the comment but I want to tell you thank you for the push.

Bishop Owens, Stacey Arielle, Leonard Siggers (NuMillenium Group), Annetta Johnson (Pleats): Thank you for allowing me to be your anchor.

Bernice Zeigler and Barbara Grayes: This one is for you!

BEING THE ANCHOR

Table of Contents

BEING THE ANCHOR

Table of Contents (cont.)

The End

Foreword

One definition of the word "anchor" is "a person or thing that can be relied on for support, stability, or security." This definition is the embodiment of the administrative assistant. No matter the industry, the administrative assistant is the anchor for the entire project.

The author of *Being the Anchor* is well qualified to express the duties and roles of being the administrative assistant because she is the anchor of B. L. Owens Ministries. Angelica Williams is the literal backbone of the administrative side of what I do. She is the glue that holds things together.

The administrative assistant's role goes beyond keeping a calendar, answering emails, writing letters or making sure meetings are attended on time. The role of the administrative assistant is to provide their CEO, manager, pastor or whomever they serve a sense of support, stability, security, and reassurance that they care for your profession as much as you do.

The administrative assistant's role or the anchor, as it is noted in this book, is all about relationship. Anyone can dress and be in place, but it takes relationship with an employer to understand their vision and bring it to life.

I am very pleased to say that after you read *Being the Anchor* not only will you know how to be an effective administrative assistant, but you will also know how to build trust and reverence for whomever you serve. I am proud to say that Angelica Williams is the anchor of B. L. Owens Ministries.

+B. L. Owens Sr.

Introduction

The Administrative Assistant's job is more than scheduling appointments, writing letters and answering phone calls. My goal is not to teach you how to write a letter or schedule an appointment. My goal is, however, to provide you with the foundation and principles on how you can be an effective administrator beyond the appointment scheduling, letter writing and the answering of phones. It is to help you become an effective servant. My goal in writing this book is to assist in training and developing you to be the best you can be in your role, making the job of your leaders easier, freeing him or her of the pressure to worry about administrative details. Your CEO, division manager, pastor or whomever you are assisting, should not have to constantly follow up on your work and discover it is incomplete. When given an assignment, your leader should be able to trust you to have it completed in the expected turnaround time. If your leader feels the need to consistently, follow up and/or redo your work, then they do not need you.

Please, understand that as administrative assistants, we are not slaves. While the job can be stressful and overwhelming, we should not be treated as such; and, we should be able to discern and use wisdom when deciding the difference between appropriate and inappropriate tasks.

I have assisted in administration in various industries - nonprofit, secular, music and church. While the fields may be different, the basic foundation and governing principles for being an administrative assistant do not change. If you take the information that I provide you and apply it, you will be successful at what you do.

Lastly, you must always remember to remain humble! Your ultimate goal as an administrative assistant should be to see your leader reach his or her goal, excel and their visions come to fruition. Accomplishing these things is the reward for a job well done.

How I Became the Anchor

January 2012 I went on maternity leave from my position as a Collections Tech with American Red Cross. I never imagined that my six weeks leave would turn into six months. During my time off, the Collections Department and union could not reach a feasible agreement with American Red Cross, so we went on strike. Consequently, I began applying for job after job and going on interview after interview only to receive no results. I could not understand why, with almost ten years of healthcare experience, I was unsuccessful at finding employment. Then, it dawned on me that not only was I looking for work in the healthcare industry, so were more than 200 other people, who were on strike like me. Now what should I do? I have a newborn, two other school aged children to care for and no income. "God", I prayed, "You have to do something and do something quick." It was at this point that I realized I seem to always want God to move quickly for me, but I had to ask myself "what have I done for Him or what will I do for Him?" Ironically, around this same time I, remember sitting in a meeting at church and my pastor saying to me "Maybe you should be taking this time to work on your relationship with God and get closer to Him."

I went home, prayed and told God "Ok, now You know I really do not want to go back to the Red Cross. If it is Your will for me to leave, then You'll make it happen." Soon, I began going to the church office during the day and shortly thereafter, I was asked by Bishop Owens, Co-Pastor of Second Ebenezer Baptist Church, to assist with his "God Did It" Conference. While being diligent in these tasks, for only a short time, I received information regarding an open position with the Cleveland Baptist Association. They were looking to hire an Executive Administrative Assistant and I decided to apply.

The strike ended in June 2012, but I was not scheduled to return to work until July. The same day I returned to work at American Red Cross, I received a call from the Cleveland Baptist Association offering me the position of Executive Administrative Assistant complete with all the benefits for which I prayed. The flexibility in my new work schedule allowed me to continue to serve as Administrative Assistant for B.L. Owens Ministries.

As a person of faith, I believe everything happens for a reason. Had my department not gone on strike, I would not have had the opportunity today to serve as anchor, starting me on the path to help you become the anchor in your role.

Being the Administrative Anchor

There is a gift, a talent in you that no one else can see except your leader, and you have been chosen to be a leader in your role as his or her assistant. I will also go as far as saying that there are strengths and skills you possess that even you cannot see, but your leader can.

Therefore, you have been called as the individual who has the respect of whomever you serve. It is imperative to always remember that as you interact with people in and out of your company, organization, department or church-- you are doing so on behalf of the leader for whom you serve.

With that, I offer the following tips that will aid you in being successful in your position as the administrative anchor in your organization.

At the end of each tip there will be an "Activity" or "Think about it" section and a section for notes. Applying these tasks will help you to develop in your administrative position. I encourage you to come back three to six months later to revisit your notes, complete the activity and think about the questions again, to see how much you have grown or stayed the same. Growth is great. Stagnation is not.

Tip #1
Be Aware of the Position's Requirements

As with any position, there are requirements for the position of the administrative assistant. These requirements are very important to consider before stepping into this role. I often tell people seeking the position that "if you cannot meet these requirements, then you may want to reconsider whether this is the position for you." If you feel you meet the basic requirements, then great! However, do not get your hopes up just yet. As you continue to read, I am pretty sure there will be some information that will cause you to say to yourself "No, this is not the position for me." No matter the industry, make sure you are willing to accept the requirements that come with the position.

Activity: Make a list below of some requirements that you are unwilling to accept. Once your list is complete, ask yourself "Are these really deal breakers or am I being unreasonable?"

Notes

_____

_____

_____

_____

_____

_____

_____

_____

_____

Tip #2
Take Your Position Seriously

You are more than a receptionist. You hold the administrative fate of the company in your hands. As the administrative assistant, you are the glue that holds every other function together and you are relied on more than you know. It is my advice to refrain from sharing the events of your personal life or your complaints about your position with your leader. Those in charge are solely focused on the daily operations of the company or organization and should not be distracted by your personal issues. When you are passionate about your position, then you will take it seriously.

Think about it: Are you able to take your position seriously? Do you have the ability to be the glue that holds a company together and still maintain a healthy work-life balance?

Notes

_____

_____

_____

_____

_____

_____

_____

_____

_____

_____

Tip #3
Always Be Ready

Ask yourself:

How can I work when I am not prepared to work?

You have heard the adage "If you are on time, then you are late." To be on time to work means arriving early.

It is unprofessional for the scheduled appointment to arrive before the office opens. To avoid this embarrassment, prepare to arrive to the office at least an hour before the scheduled appointment. When your appointment arrives, you should be settled and the appropriate office machines needed for use during your meeting up and running. Proper planning will ensure your guest is not arriving to a closed office. Be ready to greet your guest with a smile and a hand shake. It is good practice to always be prepared to enter into a meeting even if there is not one scheduled and to be prepared with new and fresh ideas.

Activity: Write down some tips and suggestions for yourself on how you can always be ready and prepared to work.

Notes

_____

_____

_____

_____

_____

_____

_____

_____

Tip #4
Be Aware of Your Boundaries

Setting boundaries is a principle that we must learn to do in our personal lives as well as our professional lives. People will take advantage of or be inconsiderate of you only as far as you allow. When clearly communicated boundaries are not set from the beginning when assuming your new role, things will eventually, take a turn for the worse. This is why a close review of the requirements of the job are very important.

As the assistant it is important that you never lose sight of the fact that you are the assistant and the professional assistant only. Should you be privy to any personal issues between your leader and his or her spouse or other family members, take caution to steer clear of any involvement, remain neutral in your interactions with those involved, and do not disclose any information you hear with anyone, especially those uninvolved in the matter.

Take this scenario for example: You are present in the office and an unpleasant argument begins. What should you do? Quietly excuse yourself and stand outside the door to divert anyone approaching the office by politely explaining the leader is unavailable at the moment. It may also be appropriate to request the visitor to come back at a later time and to assist him or her in rescheduling the appointment. This is not a time to socialize so do not stand outside of the door and hold personal conversations as you must be alert and attentive at all times.

Think about it: Do you know what the boundaries are in your workplace? Have those boundaries been crossed? How do you keep from crossing them?

Notes

_____

_____

_____

_____

_____

_____

_____

_____

Tip #5
Do Not Mix Business with Pleasure

If you are employed by a family member or work for a close family friend, separating relationships goes along with setting boundaries. You must separate personal from business. While in the workplace, your leader is not your mom, dad, aunt, uncle, or friend. They are your superior and should be addressed and respected as such.

Any time you are in the workplace, no matter the nature of the business, you should keep your interactions professional and everyone should be addressed by his or her title.

It is important to leave all personal issues outside of the workplace. Unfortunately, when you are unable to separate personal from professional, your personal issues begin to spew over into your professional work and you begin to slack in your assignments. Leave your personal feelings at the door when entering the workplace. You can be friends when you are released from your assignment for the day. Your friendship should not be negatively impacted or change based on what happens in the professional setting.

Think about it: Leaving personal feelings at the door is difficult. How do you operate at work when you are upset with your leader for something non work related?

Notes

_____

_____

_____

_____

_____

_____

Tip #6
Lower Your Expectations

If you are looking to be constantly thanked for your work as an anchor then you are in the wrong profession. This is not to say that you will not receive an expression of thanksgiving at all, but the sentiment may not be as frequent as you desire. Do not take it personally, or allow hurt feelings to show in your facial expressions or negative body language. This does not mean you are not appreciated. It just means many times, you will have to trust the confidence in yourself, your unique skill set and your leader to know your contributions are valued and appreciated.

Know that at times you will be overwhelmed and have to choose your responses carefully while feeling stressed. There will be times you will have to put on a smile and walk away; and, this may happen several times in one day. The ability to grin and bear will become second nature. But, if you do not like people, you will not succeed in this role because this position requires interaction with both internal and external customers. Your attitude will determine your success or failure. This is not the position for negative attitudes and demeanors

Activity: Write down ways you can combat your attitude and not take offense when you feel unappreciated.

Notes

_____

_____

_____

_____

_____

_____

_____

Tip #7
Confidentiality

Next to social media, confidentiality is the most important to me. Not everyone is able to work closely with the leader. You get the chance to see a different side of them as they deal with the challenges of being a business owner that cannot be shared with everyone. They are looking for someone they can be comfortable with and you have been chosen for the job.

Your leader has realized his or her need for administrative assistance and support. This position requires someone who can be trusted and this means you must be trustworthy. You must be trusted to hear, but not hear and see, but not see as you may be privy to see and hear some information that you may not like or with which you disagree. It is not your job or your position to repeat anything you see or hear, not even to your leader. This means you cannot share private information with your parents, spouse, children or friends.

You would be surprised how many people are interested in the position of the administrative assistant and you would be surprised at how many do not survive in the position once they obtain it. I tell people often that everyone cannot do this job. It is not that I am just so great at what I do. I mean, it is not difficult to manage a calendar, schedule engagements and write letters. That is the easy part of the job. The difficult part comes when you see how frustrated and upset your leader may become day in and day out.

Once again, you have been trusted to function in this role. Do not make your leader second guess the decision made to hire you. One of the biggest mistakes you can make is breaking confidentiality and losing the trust of your leader. I cannot stress enough that you only get one opportunity at being trusted and betraying your leaders' trust may be irreparable.

Activity: Write down ways you can help keep the confidentiality of your leader and the office. Do you need to close their office door when you see it unattended? Should you take your phone call into another area or at another time?

Notes

_____

_____

_____

_____

_____

_____

_____

Tip #8
Be Organized

Organization is crucial to be effective in your profession.

Develop a system and stick with it. Keep a clean workspace in order to quickly locate any documents or other important information when asked without having to search for it.

Develop your own time schedule for projects. If you are given a completion date for an assignment for the 20th of the month, be proactive by marking your submission date as the 18th of the month. Remember, if your assignment is turned in on time then it is late. You should not have to be questioned about the status of an assignment or project you have been given to do. Trust me, if you have to be questioned, that is not good. Always stay ahead of the tasks you are given to accomplish.

If you encounter an unexpected disruption and are unable to exceed or meet the deadline, be sure to communicate this as soon as possible. DO NOT wait until the due date to inform your leader you will miss the deadline and expect him or her to simply understand. Communication is imperative to your success in this position and the success of your leader.

Activity: How do you plan to keep files and assignments organized so you do not misplace documents or lose sight of the status of projects?

Notes

_____

_____

_____

_____

_____

_____

Tip #9
Dress Professionally

Acceptable work place attire is usually set by your employer, leader or industry. However, even in more relaxed work settings you must always exercise good judgement when dressing for work. If you are aware of an important meeting or special event being held or a special guest scheduled to come to the office make sure you are dressed appropriately and professionally. Pay attention to cover tattoos and to cover or remove all obvious body piercings. The following are examples of what should or should not be worn:

Men: Black or blue suit with shirt and dark colored tie with dark colored dress shoes. No jeans, shorts, cut out or sagging pants or tennis shoes. Attention to detail should be given to make sure nails are clean and well groomed.

Women: A two piece skirt or pants suit in a neutral color. Skirts should be worn with nude or black pantyhose, whichever is appropriate accompanied by appropriately colored dress flats or office appropriate heels. No jeans, shorts, leggings, cut out pants or capris or other tight clothing should be donned. Attention to detail should be given to make sure nails are clean and well groomed. Jewelry should be appropriate and kept to a minimum.

First impressions are lasting impressions. Women should take care that your first impression is not a revealing cleavage and leg exposure. Men should take care that your first impression is not an unshaven beard or mustache and sagging pants.

Think about it: What can you do to make a lasting positive first impression with your work attire and personal grooming?

Notes

_____

_____

_____

_____

_____

Tip #10
Efficiency

In order to be efficient in your position as administrator, you must possess at least a basic skill set and a working knowledge that includes, but is not limited to, personal computer literacy or word processing and power point software programs, knowledge of how to create and navigate through spreadsheets, along with organizational, records retention, prioritization and time management skills. All of these, and more, are crucial in completing your daily tasks. Without these, it is safe to say that you may want to consider a different vocation.

Make it a practice to be mindful of your response times regarding phone and email inquiries. Make it a priority to respond to all important telephone messages within two hours and emails within an hour. It is imperative to communicate status updates to callers and senders. Proper and timely communication is vital to the efficiency of your role, so it is imperative to provide status updates to your leader or manager and to both internal and external customers. This will also include at times, informing them, simply, that you are in receipt of their correspondence and will provide the necessary feedback as soon as possible. Continual failure to communicate timely and efficiently could be costly to your leader, the organization and you.

Activity: Write down ways you can improve your response time to make sure you are efficient in your position.

Notes

_____

_____

_____

_____

_____

Tip #11
Know Your Leader

It is important that you know the vision of the company, your leader and yourself. We all should have a personal vision written down. Your vision should detail where you want to go in your profession and where you want to see the company go. Do you know the vision of the company? How can you carry out the vision if you do not know the vision? If your leader gives you the vision, then you should be able to take the challenge and make the vision come alive.

Make sure your heart is in the right place. If your heart is not in the right place, it will show and be reflected in your work. If you have a hidden, ulterior motive, then this is not the position for you, and it will show.

You also must learn about your leader's preferences. Does your leader prefer that you to confirm appointments with him or her first? Does he or she want to see any correspondence before you send it out? What is his or her writing style? Get to know your leader's office habits and routines. To be an effective anchor, it is important that you identify what your leader prefers and how he or she prefers certain situations or correspondences to be handled.

Remember, everyone is entitled to a bad day including your leader. As the administrative assistant, you will need to exercise wisdom knowing how to handle those days.

Activity: Create a vision for yourself.
What questions do you need to ask your boss to understand them better professionally?

Notes

_____
_____
_____
_____
_____
_____

Tip #12
Be Mindful of Your Attitude

Your attitude is everything. You are the first line of contact for your company or organization with both internal and external customers. The experience they have with you will make the difference in retaining repeat customers or driving customers away. Make sure you have a quiet background when answering the phone and keep in mind that most listeners can hear a smile in your speaking voice even over the phone. So be sure to smile and offer a pleasant speaking tone. Stop all prior conversations when addressing customers and remember to say "please" when making requests and respond by saying "thank you". Also remember to be mindful of the tone in your emails when responding. Make sure your tone is not interpreted as coming off curt, but pleasant. It is your kind attitude, smile and professionalism that will seal the deal. I cannot stress how frustrating it is to talk to a rude administrative assistant or one who fails to respond to written correspondence. Sometimes you can learn how to do your job well, by learning from other administrative assistants what not to do. Remember you not only represent your leader, you also represent yourself.

Think about it: How has your attitude affected your work performance? How can you improve your attitude?

Notes

_____

_____

_____

_____

_____

Tip #13
Be Mindful of the Company You Keep

In work situations with more high profile CEO, managers and leaders you cannot associate with everyone. Some people will want to get close to you, simply, to get to your leader. You must remain alert, discerning and wise regarding the motives of those who try to start a relationship with you because of your administrative role.

Think about it: Do you associate with anyone that could jeopardize your position or cause issues for your leader?

Notes

_____

_____

_____

_____

_____

Tip #14
Be Respectful

You will, at times, be placed in situations that are challenging. When things turn stressful, as they sometimes will, you may bear the brunt of the frustrations of your leader, even though you may not have caused the problem. No matter how difficult or stressful challenges become, it is important to maintain a respectful attitude towards everyone. Instead of allowing the situation to get the best of you, use the opportunity to demonstrate your ability to perform under pressure and try offering solutions to resolve the matter where possible.

Activity: Write down tips and suggestions on how you can better function in and rise above a stressful situation.

Notes

_____

_____

_____

_____

_____

_____

Tip #15
Use Wise Judgement

Administrative Assistants, generally, do not work with much direction or instructions from their leader, so it is crucial for the administrative assistant to exercise sound and wise judgment in decision. If you are uncertain what decision is best when speaking with a customer, it is best to inform him or her that you will research the matter further, and provide the updated or corrected information as soon as you are able.

Wise decision making extends to your social media interactions as well. You represent your leader, manager and/or the company for which you work. As a representative, the image you reflect is important and will impact the image your customers have of your leader, the company or organization and you. Therefore, it is important that you are aware that even in an administrative assistant role, you cannot vent, share content, share your thoughts, repost, re-tweet, click like or make a comment, joke or interact with every social media post you follow or see, including on your personal social media accounts. Social media networking and marketing is always progressing which means someone will always be watching your organization's business/professional social media accounts or your personal social media accounts. It is, also, important to remember that even if something questionable is deleted, it is never really deleted forever. So, it is good practice to be proactive about what content should be posted in the first place.

Think about it: Is there anything on your social media accounts that could jeopardize your position or the credibility of the company? What things should you disassociate with or delete from your account?

Notes

_____
_____
_____
_____
_____

Tip #16
Take Initiative

A thorough administrator must learn to administrate needs before they are brought to you by your leader. If you are aware of an upcoming event that requires travel arrangements to be made, take initiative to secure the arrangements before your leader asks. This increases your leader's trust in your ability to be proactive; and, will not only enhance the efficiency of operations of the office, but also create the potential for increased responsibilities and, perhaps, promotions in the future.

Activity: Write down some upcoming needs in the office and how you can show initiative by having them accomplished prior to the deadline or your leader's request.

Notes

_____
_____
_____
_____
_____
_____

Tip #17
Believe in Yourself

It is true that if you do not believe in yourself, no one else will. A strong, but balanced belief in yourself equips you to take on tough, daily challenges. You were hired because of the company's, the organization's or your leader's belief in your qualifications to be a good fit for this role. Excessive degrading of yourself, especially if you make a mistake or an oversight, can make others feel uncomfortable and is not healthy. Therefore, refrain from doing this and make sure to always put your best self forward.

Set goals. Keep track of your progress in reaching your goals and think of ways to improve your performance because no matter how skilled or good you are in your role, there is always room for improvement. Don't be afraid to continue your education. While formal education can be costly, there are other ways to stay current with new information relating to your position. This can be achieved by doing informal research on the internet or speaking with other trusted colleagues or peers. You can also subscribe to industry publications. The key is, simply, to be committed to increase your knowledge of your craft and your industry.

Being knowledgeable about your position enables you to perform well. This will enhance your ability to excel in your administrative role. Trust that you are qualified to do the job. Your organization already does.

Activity: Write an encouraging or affirming note to yourself. Example: I am qualified to do and excel in my administrative role. I will accomplish my goals and meet deadlines.

Notes

_____
_____
_____
_____
_____

_____

Tip #18
Take Care of Yourself

The demands and challenges of any job can make even the strongest person weary or exhausted. It is no different with administrators as we take care of the daily, ever changing tasks that keep an office or business operating efficiently. Although the administrative responsibilities can be great, as with any job, it is important to schedule time away from the office for rest.

When you do not take proper care of yourself mentally, physically and emotionally, you become little good to others and jeopardize your work performance. So, it is important to maintain a healthy work, life balance, including scheduling, where appropriate, short breaks away from your computer monitor or your desk during work hours.

Activity: Write down some ways you can take better care of yourself, both inside and outside of the workplace?

Notes

_____

_____

_____

_____

_____

Tip #19
Be Encouraged

As you know, there are many challenges that you will face in an administrative position. I can recall one of the roughest months of my career and I was ready to throw in the towel. No one knew how I was feeling, but I had prepared my resignation letter. Before getting out of my car to hand in my resignation, I prayed to God, asking Him to give me a sign if this position is where He wanted me. Within an hour, I received two encouraging messages from two of my closest friends, neither of whom had any knowledge that I was preparing to resign. I kept those messages and refer to them sometimes for encouragement when I feel stressed. Grateful for having received the confirmation and reassurance I needed, then, I want to share the messages to help anyone who may be discouraged, feel like quitting, questioning if you should continue in your role or have, like me, prepared your resignation.

Message 1: *"Be still before you walk away and let everyone else win. God called you to your position, not them, not Bishop and not you. The Earth will run out of gas before you step down in this season. Endure it and laugh at their tactics."*

Message 2: *"I just want to let you know that you are doing an awesome job at what you're doing. It gets hard, stressful and people will make you mad because they judge what they don't know. But all that you're doing is not in vain. Don't flip or give up, everything is working together for your good. You just finish the race. It is not given to the strong or swift (it would be too easy) but it's given to the one that will endure unto the end. Anything easy isn't worth anything. So you keep going and keep pressing."*

These messages helped to encourage and uplift me while I was experiencing some of the toughest challenges in my career. There are moments where you may feel as if you are constantly giving and supporting everyone around you, leaving you with little time for yourself and feeling empty and underappreciated. I have felt this weight to the point of tears after many hours on the long projects and many days of constant meetings. Being misunderstood by others has made me think of quitting.

Yet, I weathered the storm and you can too by connecting with other assistants who can relate to what you may be currently, facing and offer suggestions on how best to process and deal with what you are feeling. Otherwise, you can lend support through encouraging words or sharing tips from personal experiences to ensure each of you are aware that you are not alone on this journey. It can be helpful to surround yourself with those who will encourage you when you feel overwhelmed or feel pressure to quit prematurely. Being the anchor will require you to learn how to process your feelings in a reasonable and healthy manner so that the administrative duties of your position and organization do not fall lacking.

Being able to see the fruit of your labor is one of the most rewarding feelings ever and it is what will motivate you to keep going.

Think about it: Identify some other administrative assistants from whom you can receive and for whom you can be a source of encouragement. Once you have done so, consider making plans to contact him or her to begin creating your professional support system of administrators.

Notes

_____

_____

_____

_____

_____

_____

Tip #20
Be the Anchor

Now that you have completed reading these tips, I hope you have also determined if this is, in fact, the position for you. If this is not the position for you, please do not conclude that you have wasted your time. The road to discovery is never a waste because through it you may be able to discover the profession you truly desire to pursue.

For those readers who are certain the role of administrative assistant is your call and passion, I encourage you to apply the tips I have shared so you can be the administrative anchor in your place of business, your organization, or your company.

Be the kind of administrative assistant that other administrators want to emulate. You have the capacity to be an invaluable asset by being the assistant that other companies, organizations, departments and leaders seek to use to train their pool of assistants. So, strive for excellence no matter how seemingly trivial the task.

You are the office and your leader's support and bring stability to the administrative ship. You provide the security that enables your leader to trust that you will stay on course and arrive at your administrative destination on time. So, as you start each work day, remember the importance of the administrative role because...

YOU ARE THE ANCHOR!

www.ingramcontent.com/pod-product-compliance
Lightning Source LLC
Chambersburg PA
CBHW071317280526
45788CB00004B/1928